THE CONDUCTOR'S CALL

Tom Davis

To order additional copies of this book, contact:
Xlibris Corporation
1-888-795-4274
www.Xlibris.com
Orders@Xlibris.com
37318

Contents

CHRISTMAS POEMS

GRANDSONS

MORE POEMS

FORWARD

Why publish? Why now? Some months ago, near the end of a recent year, my daughter received an email. In it the sender told of a loved one close to death. Since Christmas was near, he had recently received our card including my annual attempt at a poem with some small message to share. My daughter's friend closed his email by saying he was taking my card to the hospital to read the words to his failing mate and then he added, "how great is that!?" Just remembering reading that email still makes my chest and throat tighten up.

Words matter. Words hit people differently because their lives have traveled different paths. When a reader picks up a poem or a note or a book, the words are as much about the reader's experience as they are about the writer's intentions. None of these works presents grand new insights. My aspiration is smaller—to let the words work their magic. When I've succeeded the words can break through a personal facade, touch a soul, or tweak our brains' unexamined thoughts.

Most of what you'll find here goes after small subjects. Our friends have complemented the poems and the writer far more than is deserved. Friends are kind that way but I am always grateful to hear a bell was rung with some of my words as the clapper. To publish a book, even one as small as this, fulfills a life goal. With luck something here will justify your time to read it.

I owe great gratitude to my wife whose reactions to drafts have always led to improvements. More importantly, even with the worst of these efforts she has never refused to sign her name to the Christmas card that carried the poem.

By publishing now, I am setting these poems free. They are yours. They belong to everyone who reads them. My hope is that reading these poems will let you feel like a small puzzle piece has found its right place in your life.

CHRISTMAS POEMS

Poetry started for me at Christmas. Always fond of words and loving to read or hear words that inspire, I decided to try to share the feelings our family always felt at Christmastime. We have always been truly and greatly blessed. Our family has known great love, great joy, unflinching support, and material bounty testing our ability to keep it in perspective. With all of that, we believe that we are exceptionally ordinary people.

Each year we tried to find a way to put some small message about our experience into words. The poems are meant to tell a story or convey a feeling. In doing so, poetic conventions sometimes suffered. If there was a line or couplet or verse that touched the minds or hearts of our friends, Christmas was made merrier. Sometimes a poem's story became a way to talk about caring more for our world but none were meant to preach. They were simply a way to share our search for deeper truths and callings.

The poems in this section span about twenty-five Christmases. There have been gaps and one of the poems even speaks about hiatuses in life. Many friends have spoken kindly about how they've been touched by one or more of these verses. I hope by collecting them here you can easily revisit the ones you like and maybe discover new meaning from one long discarded. In many respects they reflect my quest to discover all the meanings of Christmas.

A Life in the Day of a Snowman

Dawn creeps into day as streaks of new light
First carving then drenching the morning sky,
The white glare announcing, this morning is snow.

If clay can be molded into vessels, and dust can be . . .
This snow will be snowmen.

Created by hands, mostly small and well mittened,
They'll populate yards and boulevard medians,
Each done with intention of creating perfection.

But some turn out fat and others will be slim
Or they'll list a little as if walking with a limp.

Adorned and attired with all manner of clothes
Each has the traditional carrot nose,
And even as new, some heads sit slightly askew.

At the zenith of sun-track, when noontime peals
More flaws and blemishes become unconcealed.

There are lumps and twigs in the muddy sphere
But at midday he's sturdy, resolute he appears
As if snowmen will last to the end of the year.

Withered at day's end, slumping to one side,
Their hats droop low and are too large in size.

But the day, what a day, an incredible high,
Touched by children with joyful, innocent eyes,
They're able to stand smiling to strangers who pass by.

The night breezes whisper as snowmen pray
Their thanks for the life lived out in one day.

A Christmas Story

"Twas the night before Christmas"—so it began
The story of Santa Claus, his elves and his friends.
But an unfaded memory in a year of my youth
Is a story then told me, I know now as truth.

"Come here lad," said the jolly old man;
The words I'd awaited, my turn was at hand.
"Come right up here, and tell me your wishes,
What do you know about why we have Christmas."

Up on his lap as I squirmed and giggled, tried
Quickly to tell him of toys I had dreamed.
Then he squeezed me with a big bear style hug
Said, "Son you've been blessed with boundless love."

"You know my boy that hundreds of years ago
A baby was born and the skies burst aglow.
This baby named Jesus, God's Son born to be—
The reason for Christmas, and for you on my knee."

"So now, little man, is the time for you to hear
The story passed down by those who were there.
This story of the gift that began as a baby boy—
Has been passed through the years—the Christmas story."

Santa had spoken but nothing about toys.
He'd never asked if I'd been a good boy.
His eyes truly sparkled as he spoke through his smile
But said nothing of elves nor reindeer wiles.

A Christmas Story (cont)

> My turn on his lap was over and done, and then,
> I crinkled my brow not sure what just happened.
> But then Santa hugged me in that way that feels right
> And I grinned and knew I'd remember that night.
>
> Now when I'm asked if Santa is real and alive
> The memory of that night puts his glint in my eye.
> I can share with authority that Santa is real.
> He delivers gifts that last through the years.
>
> As his sleigh finds its way to the heart of each child
> He's happy to bring, again and again, a Christmas smile.

Christmas' Door

Framed by the garland, the pine bough rope,
With glittering lights, the symbol of hope,
Arrivals bespoken by ringing chimes,
Come in and share this Christmas time.

This house, our dwelling, the place that we
Would share with all friends joyously,
The fireside's warmth and friendship's feelings
And thanks for His gift—Jesus' being.

An open door, the symbol we use
For opportunity—the chance to choose;
Likewise His promise brought years afore,
Depicted each year—it's Christmas' door.

With the coming of Christmas, spirits lift
And our thoughts turn to wishes and gifts.
Our family's wish for you and yours,
Is for joy, gladness, and open doors.

Consider Christmas

Consider snowflakes
Wafting down on a still winter's night.

Consider embers
Sharing the glow of their red-orange light.

Consider handshakes
Passages for friendship in strength of touch.

Consider embraces
Memories of home summoned by a clutch.

Consider dreams
Images and pictures, an ephemeral play.

Consider music
Resonating emotion as it ripples away.

Consider memories
Confirming that life is assuredly fleeting.

But consider Christmas
His promise fulfilled, constancy beating.

Crossing to Home at Christmas

Set out
> Across life's daily currents, trek to Christmas
> At home, over hills and rivers, walls and fences
> Using barges, bridges, tugs or ferries.

Wade in
> To torrents tearing through the trip-tick
> Through currents comprised of circumstance
> And filled with frenzied, frazzled friends.

Find foot-holds
> 'Tween rounded, moss-slicked, river stones
> Bumped by bleached and barkless branches
> Seek the sure-step spots in stream-bed sand.

Carry on
> When each misstep slip begets a soaking
> And often loss of things we've toted;
> Reach up and grasp a proffered hand.

Rise up
> And watch for the window glow at gloaming;
> Recall home's myth and mirth and memory.
> Refocus on the light that pierces night and

Reach back
> Clasp a hand and help another step ashore.
> We'll all have crossed to Christmas when
> The least among us has been welcomed

Home.

Endlessness Found

The truths we acknowledge and teach as right
Are manifested by the rules we often cite.
Such rules evolve into the laws we write
So our judgments will appear erudite.
While the Word is meant for each neophyte,
It's law often seems an elusive sight.
Yet the oft heard claim is it's taught aright;
And those who don't learn we're quick to indict.

A new vision is formed when we invite
Christ's truth and His passion that will ignite
Wisdom from laws of the Israelite
Remembering God as the signal light.
Of God, not humankind, are truth and right;
Ours is to learn and to follow the light.

Rules, like the poet's meter and rhyme,
Should assist us in making each day's climb.
They must never be, nor become, God's mime
Nor to judge a life in its dotage or prime.

Depicted by grapevines wreathed in a round,
Just His judgment matters, endlessness found.

Father's Hand

The pain of the night intensifies as light dims,
and life's first encounter with night pain seems bigger
than the night—alone in bed. It can make a little one cry.

But just at the instant of my short life's sharpest
jolt of pain, one large and time hardened hand hangs
over the bed rail and reaches down to engulf

My little bundle of cold trembling fingers.
"Squeeze," was commanded by that sonorous bass
voice, reverberating in whispers; so obeying,

I do. And the sharp, prickly thorns of night pain
withered; less in that moment, than in the knowing
that soon such pain would ebb away in memory.

I remember the feel of the cracked and calloused skin
of my father's hand, and how, in one firm squeeze,
pain could not compete with the security of his touch.

Each of us is often given the chance to proffer
our old time hardened hands to children who need us,
but as they reach urgently up, most fail to be grasped.

His children, we, some Christmases ago placed
all our pain in His Right Hand and He carried pain
away. It's our time, our call, to reach out and squeeze.

Mind The Gap

At Victoria Station for the Tube under London,
"Mind the gap" in mechanical tones drones on and on.
Not "watch your step" nor simply, "take care,"
Over the inch or two from platform to subway car.
The message surrounds every passenger passing here.
Some listen, some don't, some hear and some won't.
Uncommon counsel, unerringly dispensed for
Renewing connections that have been let lapse.

Of time, of distance, of loss, or perception,
Gaps that need minding tend to be

Not minutes, but months since marking the moment
        when daily discussion dissolved into memories
        and touching transitioned to talking of touching.
Of despairing about that which we haven't
        instead of decrying for those who really don't.
Of knowing what's right but doing the familiar,
        forgoing the pebbled path, opting for pavement.
Impassioned opining of facts coyly clothed,
        employing flim-flammery data fettering truth.
Prefabricated memories, dashed by the real
        as the joy of the moment passes unknown.
Time's constant lapsing to everlong gone, when
        words that could have been spoken or penned,
        were not—an absence belying intent and thought.

Words wend their whisper deeply within—
Mind the gap, hear the silence,
See the crevice, feel the void—and find,
In the gaps, this Christmas, is where He resides.

Innocence

Pristine.
>Night snow repaints the world pristine.
>Youthful mornings are for being first
>to sully such snow with tracks and angels,
>snowmen and snowballs. And

Outside,
>her hood-string is chin biting, but
>time has come to waddle on. "Stay close,
>there are coyotes about." "Mom always worries,
>but I'm big for a girl of six." With

Treats,
>she walks and skips clumsy in snow.
>It is fun alone with the snow. Pockets full
>of Mom's special treats; here comes the
>queen of her castle white. To the

Field.
>"Off I go—I'll be careful and not stay too
>long. I won't get lost. I'll just follow
>back my tracks. Pretty smart, that's what
>Grandpa always says." New

Tracks.
>First hers. Then crossing her path behind,
>different tracks; not boot-tracks, not
>shuffling, not sliding; smaller, a custom
>mold with five pads, four toes. Certainly

Stalking.
>Back and forth, paths intersecting, a tightening
>spiral. Warily closer, now clearly stalking.
>She spins and his yellow stare
>captures her innocent gaze. Frozen

Innocence (cont)

Time.

    Seconds transform into crisp winter air.
    First movement is hers, a smile; she
    proffers one of Mom's special candies. He
    bares his teeth; she giggles, drops the piece. He

Strikes.

    Scooping the treat, he retreats to the nearby
    trees. She journeys on. He returns.
    She offers candy and taking it from her
    hand, he's gone. Again and again and

Again.

    Impatiently this time he charges and drives
    his snout deep in her pocket. She raps
    him firmly, squarely on the nose. "No,
    no,—bad boy! Wait your turn." And

Then.

    "One for you and one for me." She
    giggles, he shuffles; side by side, they travel.
    Marking the passing time is only snow
    And tracks and the supply of treats. Until

Finally,

    With hands spread and arms akimbo, she
    says, "All gone!" Sadness rings in her voice
    as her forlorn eyes lock with his. He charges—
    brushes her side, spins and sprints away. She's

Home. "Hi Mom!"

    Innocence and snow—perhaps prerequisites
    for sharing treats with one who would
    rather feast on you. Such trust cannot be simply
    summoned and often melts sooner than snow. One

Christmas,

    The lions will lay with lambs, and the little
    children's innocence will not melt as they
    become the adults who feed the hungry,
    from their own pockets—without fear.

Innocence is pristine.

Of Prayer On Mountaintops

Climbing a mountain is daunting indeed.
The effort must come from deep inner need.
The air there is thin and breath hard to draw,
And speaking emits sounds like a raspy caw.
       All that remains is to hear the breeze sing.

As in such a place, Christ repaired to pray,
Imagine if He were just human that day,
Breathless and unable to speak a word,
No petition uttered, nothing spoken to be heard.
       Panting for breath, He could only listen.

Perhaps as He walked and, among us, taught,
Our noise of praying drowned that which He sought,
And climbing the mountain was done to teach,
That the act of prayer was hearing, not speech.
       Perhaps the mountain was singing—hear, here!

Christmas Trumpet

Arriving after riding long upon the winter wind,
The trumpet's haunting, minor-key notes riffle
The strings of the instrument that is our soul, and
Each crisp tone awakens images deeply stored—

A dust-laden soldier systematically
Working the streets of a distant, hostile place;

Or a woman clutching her child and waving from her
Roof, surrounded by the eddies of sludge filled flood;

Or a baby curling his tongue to make new sounds
And grinning at the applause such sounds evoke.

Perhaps you see a sleigh, bedecked with bells
And filled with a bulging bag of toys;

Or a homeless man in a tattered coat pulled tight
Who held up his hand, but his eyes looked down;

Or the empty living room of the apartment where
A mom and dad and a Downs child made do.

As the Christmas trumpeter's satin tones summon the
Images that made us think and made us feel, we've known
Great blessings. For we, so blessed, much work remains—
He calls us to attend to the resonating strings of our soul.

Probably

Driving eastbound, early—before dawn.
Sleepy and grumbling
about having to work on Christmas Eve.
The vaporous predawn light closes behind
and leaves no trace of my passing.
Such light portends daybreak,
but feels like endless nightfall.
Dreary old day.
Vapors spin in the clouds—
Nature's prerequisite for sentimental snowfall.
It will come before this day ends.

Off in the distance,
right in the middle of the road—a light,
looks to be hanging.
Probably a plane.
Tires burnish the asphalt ribbon
joining chorus with the radio twaddle
to anesthetize my mind.
Time elapses, miles traversed,
yet, it's still there.
Probably a helicopter,
or weather balloon or
single engine plane.

Probably (cont)

So, am I following the road
or the light?
Wonder what it is—I'd like to
follow it;
If I had time,
If people wouldn't think me strange.
Probably a . . . I can't this time.

It disappeared.

What it probably was,
it might not have been.
Wise men must be
wise enough
to follow—rather
than try to explain such lights.

The snow came.

Suffer Unto Him

Once, not when, the legend goes. On
This day the winter sun rose low, and
A father, two daughters and a puppy dog
Sallied out on a daylong expedition to the woods.
With new snow—the plan,
To build a snowman, of the ordinary kind,
To stand visible, vigilant, at this place, for this time.
Dad's job; carry the tools and the attire.

Sculpting with snow is kids' work performed
Under innocent eyes, my mittened touches.
In memory's time, an instant elapsed
And sure enough, Dad forgot the hat.
Though bedecked with a scarf and large carrot nose,
The snowman's smile left a lugubrious look,
Brought on by bare-headedness and nearby sad eyes.
Dad promised he'd bring the hat back.

He returned to the woods alone the next day, and
Unless he was lost, their snowman was gone.
Tossing the hat on the spot he thought right
He shrugged and wondered, but ambled on home.
A warm week ensued, but Saturday brought
A new coverlet of snow and the girls cried out,
"To the woods, let's go!!" "Okay, but
Your snowman has probably melted away."

Suffer Unto Him (cont)

Then, through the trees, atop last week's spot,
Stood their snowman. His hat rested low
At a jaunty rake and his full, broad smile
Completely effaced his crestfallen cast.
The day, filled with play, made memories
'Til time to go, when the girls ran ahead, and
Dad glanced back; just to see it once more.
But all he could see was a forest of trees.

The Flood Of . . .

Twenty-two. Sitting on the bank, all is well.
Twenty-six. It's still raining. More predicted.
Thirty-one. It will crest, if there's no more rain.

Flood. A simple word for waters rising.
Visibly persistent, undaunted and patient,
Nature prevails over man's efforts at control.
Futility gushes where levies had been,
Ruing lost wisdom while it's flooding again.
Inexorably flowing from sources to mouths,
Through the channels cut by torrents and trickles.
Rivers fed by rain-soaked streams, brooks and creeks,
Carve out new channels at the flood's behest.

Thirty-eight and rising. Will the levy hold?
Forty-two. How high, how high? My God, how high?
Forty-nine. No rain for three days. It's crested!

With all kinds of swill flushed into her channel,
Cleansing the river is the duty of floods.
And a wrong is righted, disrespect reproved.
The mud of the flood covers all and all things,
Besmirches without favor, without esteem,
Blots out all artifice of wealth or station,
Leaves everyone covered, no blemish, no fame.
Mud buries the prejudices, which keep us
From sharing, from sympathizing . . . from helping.

Forty-one. Mud invades every crevice.
Thirty-four. It's all right to cry.
Twenty-seven. It's time to try.

The Flood Of . . . (cont)

> Educated by water and cleansed by mud.
> We'll long remember this year of the flood.
> We've given a hand to one another and
> Now it's time to renew, to rebuild, and
> To relearn the lessons taught by nature.
>
> Twenty-two. On the bank, it's peaceful,
> We're calm and blessed.

The Narrow Way

We've been instructed, gently and clearly,
On life's journey, go the way narrowly.
Youthful confidence sallies forth seeking
The narrow path, Christ's subject of teaching.

Embarking the path, the obvious way,
Others walking there, confirming the way,
Some turning, some stopping, some just fell away,
It seemed they'd rejected the narrow way.

My judgment was harsh, observing their path,
They've strayed, if I've stayed, on the narrow path.
Judgment of others is never a right,
But this is the one path, chasing the light.

During every journey, there comes a time,
Fatigue and confusion obscure the line.
Whenever unsure of which path to take,
Remember the mountain, pray and awake!

The path is lost Lord, indeed it is gone;
It was glistening wet pavement lit by the moon,
'Til clouds rolling through, dodging in and out,
Let moonlight reveal the wyes in the route.

Immersed in the map's webs, searching for home,
Brought to mind The Path-Way, a truthful tome'
Tales of the Path, man's contrivance to judge,
Surrounding the Way, God's gift as we trudge.

Talents abounding, one path can't fit all.
Walk each path narrowly answers the call.
Not a lone path came that first Christmas Day,
But His truth for all paths, "I am the way."

There Is A Time

The pace is calm, almost peaceful, when viewed from afar,
The downward progression is steady, harmonious, coordinated;
But observe each grain closely in its unfaltering pursuit,
And the general calm is betrayed by the stress to be first.

In the upper globe, the number of grains inexorably dwindles,
And the pace of the chase seems to quicken toward frenzy,
'Til the final grain plunges through the crystal neck
Crashing down on its brethren in marking time's end.

The last grain cannot mark the end of time for it is first,
Awaiting only a turn to lead the way in a new beginning.
It is the promise of Christmas that's renewed as He wraps
His fatherly hands around the timeless glass and—it turns.

And last is first, and old is new, and end is beginning.
And through his grace—the pace is calm, almost peaceful . . .

The Storyteller

One Christmas Eve several years ago,
We were playing games together so
Intensely—we didn't know,
A man was watching but stood alone.

He was so still it was quite a time
Before we knew he had joined our line.
Then he said in a soft spoken line,
"Come my children for it's story time.

We gathered round him just as he'd asked,
Quickly moving, our excitement masked.
We sat in stillness, attention clasped.
None of us knew him—none of us asked.

His story began—a rising star
A magnificent light—globular.
Blade of light free of its scimitar,
Then mental sounds—tintinnabular.

The light and the ringing were the sign
Of the birth of a babe now divine;
Promise of joy and love will incline
To those who know Him throughout time.

Thirty years passed as the boy grew;
He studied the word until He knew
The time to answer, His call ensued—
Ministry of love, first with a few.

The Storyteller (cont)

Numbering twelve, they were common men,
But in Him they found truly a friend.
Together they traveled, learned to send
Word of His teachings and what He meant.

Miracles engulfed the faithful fold,
Mysteries of life His stories told;
His flock now gathered—a hundredfold,
To come to know Him as friends of old.

Then came the time—the appointed hour,
Departure time—ascend the tower.
Followers wept, their friend's final hour;
They believed His death, the ending hour.

The sun rose three times after the end,
Then He rose in life, there to ascend
To join His Father, life without end
And returned to be ever their friend.

The story ended, our trance was deep,
It was as if we'd all been asleep.
Slowly we roused, returned to the game
All sort of dazed—also aflame.

We finished the game wondering if
The Storyteller had been in our midst;
Though not one voice chose to question this,
Memories recall hearing, "Yes He is!"

Walls and Borders

Distant beginning, rumble, rumble,
    Ragtag gathering, jumble, jumble;

Now onward traipsing, rumble, rumble,
    Voices discoursing, grumble, grumble;

Momentum gaining, rumble, rumble,
    People are speaking, mumble, mumble;

Respite alluring, rumble, rumble,
    Despot decaying, fumble, fumble;

Jagged and breaking, rumble, rumble,
    Brick mortar twining, tumble, tumble;

Freedom is quaking, rumble, rumble,
    Borderlines fading, scumble, scumble;

Decibels rising, rumble, rumble,
    Those once confining, stumble, stumble;

Aftershocks wracking, rumble, rumble,
    Border walls cracking, crumble, crumble;

Prince of Peace coming, rumble, rumble,
    We could be learning, humble, humble;

    Be humble, humble;

    Be humble.

GRANDSONS

This section is brief and it is actually a subset of the Christmas poems. It is a very special subset. These three poems were written in the years of birth of our three grandsons. As every grandparent knows, there is no feeling so unique as that generated by a grandchild.

The years since their births have given me more material than I'll ever be able to write. It reminds me every day that the true poets of this world are parents and grandparents. Children are the greatest poems ever written.

Finnian James

A rainbow can dance when it has reason for joy.
Its dance is like moonlight on a rippling stream,
But its time is the day—whether midday or three.
Sometimes it climbs through the folds of gray clouds
Or rides on the vapors of aftermath mists
From passing by showers or day-long rain.

Watch the fingers of the bass player's hands
As they spring and jump in a jazzy dance.
The left runs up the great neck to fret, so the right
Can pluck the strings and elicit those deep-throated
Sounds from the sonorous bass—to join the mist from
The bass-man's sweat—urging newborn rainbows to dance.

One fine, May day for rainbows and bass-men,
At three on the second, brought Finnian James.
The Bandleader had needed an Irish named lad
Imbued with rainbows and leprechaun's love.
The gig is to play the Bandleader's tunes and to
Color gray skies by helping rainbows to dance.

Finn's search for his music, his place and his path, will
Draw on Dad's depth and Mom's rainbow smile.
His life may share the rhythm of an unseen drum
But his day will come to play in the band—to
Accompany the bass when the Bandleader counts
So the beat and the tune will inspire rainbows to dance.

The Mason

The Foreman stepped back, surveyed the site.
He issued the call for a craftsman to come.

Forty weeks hence, the prayer was answered
A son, a brother, a grandson—new stones.

Now comes a mason to lay his corner and
To build, piece by piece, stone by stone.

Each resting upon the last,
Supporting the next—and all that follow.

To prepare the stone, the mason is taught
To saw or score, to split, or hammer-hew

Freshly sawn slabs born as river rocks.
His eye and sinew must coordinate to cut

Every edge, every shape to artfully fit—a
Pier or a wall for each of life's stories.

Once shaped, each stone must be laid
Truly, squarely, plumb in its place.

String lines and trowels, levels and squares,
Tools may be your hands, but

The Mason (cont)

Building follows the Foreman and the art
Of seeing, of feeling, of trusting your heart.

To each apprentice who aspires to the craft
Dawns the marvels of each stone's traits—

Its colors and shape, the strength of its weight and
How every stone fits when he builds its space.

Thomas' Train

Welcome aboard my little lad!
I'm mightily glad you've joined us.
The Conductor chose this train for you,
(He knows about riders, rails and routes)
So adventure awaits us all and always.

As with John Henry's hearty hammer, helped
By gangling, graceful gandy dancers,
Your folks have surveyed sites and set
The track—where you'll be giggling and growing—
And learning over miles eclipsed, end by end.

Dad and Mom have made your home
A comfortable compartment.
They fuel the firebox and free your fetters, so
You rest when rocked by railroad rhythms
And can confide in the Conductor.

There'll be stations set astride the rails,
They're signaled slow for stops. There'll be
Passenger platforms with placards posting
Time and trains to take to places, to
Life's landmarks lain along the line.

Thomas' Train (cont)

My train has traveled time and miles.
More miles behind than lie before me,
But I believe each platform has a bench
Where we will meet with time to share
Candy bars or cinnamon cakes and talk.

We'll listen for the loco' whistle.
We'll heed the Conductor's call.
We'll ride on trains whose separate routes
Are joined by love and journeys shared—
All Aboard.

MORE POEMS

In this final short section of the book are a few poems covering several styles and subjects. I found doing this type of writing to be some of the most difficult work I have ever done. Each of the poems in this group has been revised—some dozens of times. All of them could, and might be, revised again.

Ideas for the kind of poem found in this section start with a feeling generated by something I've seen. Usually a small phrase or an unusual description comes to mind and that seed grows into a series of thoughts. I jot the lines in a rapid scrawl and later try to see if there is some form that fits the idea. Revising starts then. In some cases, entire poems have been discarded but the idea stayed in my head only to reemerge later.

This group of poems, and other similar poems that were left out of this book, can stay in my notebooks and files for years. I'll come back, read the notes, the drafts and the last version. I do this with even the few that have been published before. Revisions almost always jump to mind. This makes me believe that some poems may never be done.

With that said, I decided it was important to include a small representation of non-Christmas works in this book. Many of my friends are not Christian, for others religion is not important in their lives, but many have still found resonance with the poems in our Christmas cards. I believe that every poem can touch someone. Poems should aspire to find the common nobility in our humanity. I hope the inclusion of this last group of poems will contribute to that cause.

One Yellow Rose

With one yellow rose, I asked you to dance.
You couldn't know then if the music would last.
Could we dance down the wind—hands tightly clasped,
Through canyons on mountain tops, mile upon mile?
Three decades and five—it's only time and
Ours is a slow dance of the sock hop kind.

Our two hearts have beat a billion times each
And our rhythm and steps have been mostly in sync.
We've danced to the Drifters, saved snowmobile smiles.
We've loved and begat—and created new loves.
Now again, with one yellow rose and a slow dance song,
Will you continue this dance while the music goes on?

An Alternate Route

I.

The wind slid down from Canada
As fast as a bobsled in a dead straight run
And collided with humid-heavy air
Riding the back-side of the low over New Mexico.
These weather masses roiled for hours—into days.
Such rare violence closed the Interstate road.
Home, for now, lay at the end of an alternate route.
With an hour gone and, given luck, a dozen more to go,
We crested a hill at forty and there ahead appeared,
Eleven bison, pure white, marching toward us
Up the roadside curve in regimental single file.
Four, then a gap, then seven more, heads low
But resolute, their pace suggested an infinite march.
When the wind lifted and swirled the bone dry snow,
The visage of the cattle would come, then be lost,
As a single pixel fades into nature's infinite screen.

II.

A distant eye could watch us, in our automobile,
Appearing to streak on with purpose and resolve,
Converge with this queue of stone white beasts
Whose tortoise pace and rhythmic walk showed
They knew resolve as an innate humble spirit.
We watched them march much longer than
The time it takes to read another billboard sign
Enticing us off an exit to again delay our e.t.a.

An Alternate Route (cont)

We stared transfixed as time halted to pay homage
As one led and each, except the first, went behind the
Former, and each, but the last, led the next one.
There was no contest to be first, to lead them all,
And no head hung lower at column's end.
Each profile looked like a single image cut
Then pasted eleven fold on the gray-white screen
Upon the snowy shapes of the landscape in disguise.

III.

So regular was the rhythm and
Consistent was the cadence,
I craned my neck to hear that distant trumpet
That they must hear call the pace of each hoof fall.
I wondered about the gap. Had one's march ended
Before the time when nature would demand he lead?
Were those behind the gap just laggards or
Had their strength begun to wane and they couldn't
Keep the pace? Were they feeling the cost
Of so many hoof prints already cut
In the grass and mud that lay behind?
Or were those final seven young and gaining
Ground as they closed in on the elder four?
Were all of them following the mapquest route
Etched in instinct, or did one know where he
Was going and the others knew to trust him?

IV.

If we could have walked up to their faces
Would they have shown us more—in their eyes
Or in leathery wrinkles etched deeply by years
Of leaning forward to confront the icy wind?

An Alternate Route (cont)

If there had been a news reporter embedded
In their formation, would there be answers—or
Would the questions be drowned amid the noise?
Would they be invisible in the cacophony of white?
I wonder what questions would have joined
The cob-webbed corners of a road numbed mind
If this sailing wind and roiling snow had not
Conspired to blow us to an alternate route?

For one last look, I took a glimpse into the
Rear view mirror hoping to see the marching bison—
And to find answers. What I saw were eddies of snow
That for just about a nanosecond, marked my passing.

Northwest of Wolcott

Above the tree line, touch the sky, listen
For the trumpet of a bull elk wail as it
Echoes down the silent slopes' ragged rifts.
The low arc angle of the autumn sun
Backlights the sage to a sulfurous burn
And draws windrowed shadows down into dark.
Aspen leaves ride up on thermal lifts and
Tumble to places where daylight first rose
'Til trapped by a crevice the sun couldn't warm.
Sunlight's last whisper cedes control of the dark
To the stars, embellishing an infinite sky,
Whose time burns out sending light to an eye.

Tomorrow's Plan

Dining together, Wee and me, on that
Mellow evening, not late, but moonless dark.
Cool, yet not as cold as January should be.
Ours was simple talk, with only a word,
Perhaps a phrase, a nod or a touch, or
A curled brow above a smallish smile.
Our concerns lay cloistered deep.

To allay concern for a little while,
We called to check on Dad's condition
To the nurse-on-call who nursed—who cared.
Her report brought a cheering omen—
He's been a bit cantankerous tonight.
Some comfort came from another day when he
Wielded wily grins mixed in wit-wise banter.

Relaxed a bit, we returned to quiet talk,
To one last cup of dark coffee with cream.
To tomorrow's plan for a christening—
For the baptism of Mason, our grandson
Who gives untroubled grins amid family clatter.
Tomorrow would be carefully planned for
Dedicating and celebrating his new life.

The quiet joy of making plans was
Interrupted by hollow clanging electronic tones,
Announcing an incoming call, caller unknown.
A call not meant for small talk, nor to ask—
To tell. Please hurry for he is hovering near
The edge and may have crossed over once—
We felt a tearful tipping to tomorrow's plan.

Tomorrow's Plan (cont)

The light of the morning drove out the dark but
The long night ended as the sun rose without Dad—
A feat I never considered could possibly be.
Just hours before, as we talked together, he said,
Soon, very soon, he would be heading home.
We couldn't know that tomorrow's plan called for
Old Grandpa to spend the day as Mason's new angel.

Three days

As if the stage manager called the cue—
Just as their minivan, well loaded with videos,
Toys, milk and treats,—and grandsons—
Disappeared in the east bound lanes,
The snowfall came.

Yesterday and the days before were
Filled with activity upon activity.
A walk around the block became
An expedition of discovery—of
Snow balls, barking dogs and new limits,
Of how snow looks when it melts
And of rivulets creating sculptures
And map-like designs on the ground.
New toys gave new challenges to figure
Ways to use them that surpassed
Any plan the designer may have had.
Brother's toys are not so hard when
He gets to play them in his own way.

High in the mountains where,
Snow and cold are welcomed,
On these days the sun beamed through.
Ball caps and sunglasses were the
Dress of the day. Evenings gave
Way to mittens and stocking caps
And seeing your breath all the time—

Three days (cont)

Like the mist a boy can make on
The sliding glass door to draw in.
Yogurt, straight from the cup,
With the spoon in his own hand, and
Discovering a sliver of independence
And seeing the joy in his Mama's eyes.

The warmth of those little smiles,
And the memories of simple days,
Takes the chill out of falling snow
And lets light burst through the
Gray, overcast sky.

Memories

In may only be but one day a year—
Certainly no more than a few, when
As the sun begins its evening ritual
Of streaking the sky with ribbons wide
And tapering to points in the distant east.
Such shafts strike the tenacious autumn leaves
Already painted with orange and gold,
Deep burgundy and red, with some green
Clinging to the final vestiges of summer.
Their reflections shimmer upon the lake
Dancing through the prism's colors,
To mold shapes that rise and pass, as if
The future lies upon the water's surface
And in its depths, rests the past.

King & 3rd, Alexandria

When the temperature
Hovers near freezing
And the wind is fresh,
A tailpipe plume rises
To dance a waltz or
A prom night slow dance.
The edges of the vapor
Caress the paving bricks—
As a lover may savor
The smooth contour of her neck.
Watching through the wavy
Ripples of the float-glass pane,
Plumes jive to the cacophony
Out on the time rubbed road.
It's a cobblestone street
Where men have spit,
Horses were burdened,
Generations have trod,
And a country was born.

Deserted

The remnant gravy dribbled down and dried
On rims of pottery plates, entwined to be
A short-lived sculpture in the kitchen sink.
Flatware has the duty—shore up the stack sir, each
A weary soldier needing a bath and a bed.
But table banter runs along—talk just rambles on.
The simple, idle talk of kinfolk gathered is
The fare of families without soldiers, or for
Those who desert the dishes and leave them
Unwashed and away from their home place.

Public School Door

A huge heavy door stands
Just your arm's length away,
And beneath your shoes
Is a mat, "welcome", it says.
Over this threshold you can
Find knowledge—leave fear,
Just know you are worthy to
Enter because you are here.

Working Stones

To prepare, the skillful stonemason can saw,
Or score and split,
His sediment striped sandstone blocks,
Or chip, or hammer-hew,
Diamond sawn slabs born as river rocks.

He's taught that his eye and sinew coordinate
To cut every edge to properly fit
In a dry stack design—for a wall—
Okay, a wall, but a safe place to climb, to
Be scaled by boys for scores of years.

Shaped stones are laid truly, squarely, and plumb.
String lines and trowels, levels and squares,
Tools may be his hands, but
Building flows from the plans and the art
Of seeing, feeling, of trusting his heart.

The facet of skill that goes untaught to each
Apprentice who aspires to the craft
Dawns as he marvels at each stone's traits—
Its colors and shape, the strength of its weight and
How every stone fits if he builds the right space.

To My Grandsons

Rise up boldly, humbly to the light.
Boys who become gentlemen rarely
Rue the actions of the day at night.

Generosity never erodes valuable stores
—By giving hours, help and care, you can
Rise up boldly, humbly to the light.

The need to win each skirmish outright can
Control your day and cause your conscience to
Rue the actions of the day at night.

For what you give—love, guidance or sight—
Make no condition of return or petition, just
Rise up boldly, humbly to the light.

Work is a passion that may possess and excite,
But if it never owns you, sleep well, you won't
Rue the actions of the day at night.

Advice from an old man who's risen, rued, and fallen,
Who loved you before you rushed headlong here,
Is rise up boldly, humbly to the light
And you'll not rue the actions of the day at night.

Go For The Laugh

Gathering in this place, people are bound together
By a gauzy web of images and memories,
Of laughter and of sometimes being brought to tears.
The tunes and words swallowed by the clouds and scrims
Are enriched by every new voice and instrument sound.
This place, this Lyceum, has revealed herself to be
A lover of compelling kindness and fidelity. To watch
As Philip danced with her, gave life to loving.
When he was here, he and this Lyceum united—
Love given and received by each—measure for measure.
A sinister virus may have immigrated—unwanted and alien—
To take up residence in Philly's being, but this Lyceum is
Where Philly came to hold the curse at bay with joy, gaiety,
A half-full Q-T mug, camaraderie, and laughter.
Always—Laughter.

Each visit was renewal—as though his blood coursed
Through the timbers, curtains, scrims and paint of this place—
And was cleansed—before returning to Philly's veins
Giving youthful energy and renewed hope.
Time elapses at a pedestrian pace on the streets and wooden
Walks of The Rock. In this place, the virus seemed to know
That it couldn't compete where fear was absent and time was savored
One smile or one laugh at a time among friends.
His skill was teaching—actors to see, to hear, and to
channel the emotions of life into that room, hidden in the
Recesses of the mind, where wisdom resides.
He taught audiences that an epic can be written in a single line
And epiphanies are brought on by a move, a pose or a look.
His breath brought this Lyceum to life and her walls
Remember every line and gesture, every laugh and tear.

Go For The Laugh (cont)

Now, dear friends of Philip or Philly, let your eyelids
Grow heavy and fall shut. Tilt your head a few degrees back
So you, too, can connect. Now your mind will see through the
Proscenium and into the ether, like a dry ice stage fog.
There—just there! You can see him Now!
His limbs are pretzeled in an hilarious pose, and atop that
Body is a contorted mug with eyes a-grin and shining.
Go ahead and chuckle, and, if your inhibitions will stand aside,
You'll give him one more belly laugh out loud.
Later—back stage—that will make him smile.

Moon Share

The moon at this time,
Late, before the small
Hours of a new day,
Sailed low in the sky
Laying east but south.
Surely a witch's moon
That glows deep orange
Like light from a dying fire
And cut by dark clouds hurrying
To gather into thunderheads
Who'll meet the morning
With noise and rain.
My road curls through and around
Farms and fields far from the
Aura that hovers over the city
In the night hours before a rain.
I think of you, peacefully sleeping,
And so I do not call but
I wish we chould share this moon
In case I die before getting home.

Eagle Waiting

In the aerie—there, just below the tree line
She angled her beak down close to her breast.
Her eyes remained transfixed by willing out
Her instinctive wariness of unknown dangers.
Her wings circled the nest—a protective cloak;
No olive branch nor arrows were in her talons.

Focused on a bluish-white orb that rested
In her nest and under her constant gaze,
The language of her body and her face spoke
A mother's concern and dread for the object
Of her attention. Through a powerful scope
The glint in her eye looked almost like a tear.

Waiting, waiting, waiting. Waiting for her charge
To hatch in humility and peace—to live and soar
And teach seeing the world through an eagle's eye.